COLD TO CLOSED

Written by

Frank Bravo

Copyright © 2020 by Frank Bravo

All rights reserved. No part of this book may be used or reproduced by any means, graphic, electronic, or mechanical, including photocopying, recording, taping, or by any information storage retrieval system, without the written permission of the publisher except in the case of brief quotations embodied in critical articles and reviews.

Dedication

This book is dedicated to a few important people in my life. Val, for the unwavering support and belief in me.

Long, for always being there for me. Every. Single. Time! I can never thank you enough for your support, guidance, your willingness to put your neck on the line for me.

Tony, for giving me a good dose of bitter reality and tough love. Robin, for your wisdom and wit, the conversations were always an experience!

Mom and Dad, I love you! Please know because of you, I am the person I have always wanted to be!

Table of Contents

Part One: Before You Call 1
   How to Call 2
   4 Mistakes to avoid when calling 4
   29 Laws of calling 8
Part Two: The Scripts 10
   Script 1: Immediate Follow Up 11
   Script 2: Second Style Follow Up 13
   Script 3: My boss says, who do you know that wants to take 15
   Script 4: Leaving a Voice mail x4 17
   Script 5: Let's put a face to the name 19
   Script 6: Circle of influence people that you know 21
   Script 7: Take me off your call List 23
   Script 8: Elevator script, A.K.A. asking for sales anywhere 25
   Script 9: Are you selling? 27
   Script 10: Second sale 29
   Script 11: Let's see if we can Save you Money 31
   Script 12: Why haven't you purchased our product or service yet ... 33
   Script 13: In home presentation or B2B Presentation 35
   Script 14: Customer is comparing the competition 37
   Script 15: Asking for Referrals 40
   Script 16: Asking for Referrals continued 43
   Script 17: Calling referrals 45
   Script 18: Recruitment 47
   Script 19: Recruitment continued 49
   Script 20: Reset an appointment that was canceled 51
About the author 53

Part One

Before You Call

How to Call

During every script

Sales reps can use any of the following scripts to close a sale, set appointments or move their customers to the next step forward towards closing a deal. These scripts can be used for any sales industry.

Just remember whatever response you give your clients, make sure your response has a call to action weather they accept or deny your services or products. This call to action can be either asking to set an appointment, give more information about the product or services, or simply go in for the close.

Call to action = Asking for something or guiding your customer towards something

Types of call to actions

- Asking for the appointment
- A s king for the sale
- Asking for referrals
- Guide the customer to watch a video
- Guide the customer to read an article or email
- Inviting the customer to a customer appreciation event or meeting

Understanding the scripts

When "example" is used, "example" will represent the script that you personally will be using in your cold and sales calls. Any time there's (EXAMPLE) this is designed for you to enter your own name company product and/or service in the script to make it your own based on your Product and OR service that you sell or offer and then close for the appointment or the SALE.

Here is an actual Example on reading and using the scripts

Sales Pro: Let me ask you what (Service provider do you have?)
In the following 20 scripts when you see ( ) incorporate your sales product offer or service that you provide into the (Section)

(Your product what you sell, or offer goes here)

The Truth about phones in relation to sales

Serious buyers call in and value their time which is why the prefer calling people who value their time typically can afford to buy your product. People who have all day and time to kill typically don't have a job or can't afford your product or service. So remember when customers call in they are wanting to remove themselves from the pressure of your particular sales environment and they also want to save time. They prefer to gather initial data over the phone that they need to make a well-informed decision for themselves remember they are seriously considering buying your product and or service.

With phones you can reach more customers in a shorter period of time rather than waiting on fresh traffic.
Most salespeople are not using the phone so the opportunity to shine is at its greatest.
Sales pros do make deals by making sales calls if it has not worked for you its because you did not have a well-formed process or script in other words a road map.

4 Mistakes to avoid when calling

#1 When speaking with anyone remember the most powerful four words Who Do You Know?
Whether or not somebody is interested in doing business with you, or not. Remember just because they are not interested does not mean that they don't possibly know someone who may be interested. So, make sure to ask for referrals from everyone even if they did not do business with you.

#2 Sorry you have the wrong number

Suppose when making your calls you hear sorry you have the wrong number. Now what? Here's how you can handle this and still flow into your offer or script. (Example call) lets skip ahead to the part where they say

Customer: I'm sorry but you have the wrong number.
Sales Pro: okay no problem, Mr. Mrs. customer, just to verify I called your phone number which is (123) 456-7890 is this correct?

Customer: that's correct.

Sales Pro: Okay well just so you know, (ABC Internet) has applied and attached (huge discounts and reward points or rebates or special interest rates whatever you want to say) to this phone number and it cannot be changed. This almost never happens! Let me ask you this... what (Internet service provider do you currently have?) and then from here continue into your script

or
A different sales scenario
It would be in your benefit to take advantage of it!

(what kind of vehicle do you drive?)

OR
This is a great opportunity
(do you rent or own)?

#3 Leave a voicemail

Most salespeople don't leave a voicemail. So if you leave a voicemail, you're already standing out from those who don't! Remember when leaving a voice mail to repeat your name once in the beginning and once at the end of the the voicemail that why the customer does not have to replay the entire message just to remember your name to call you back. In addition repeat your call back number twice as well towards the end of the voice mail It's also important to speak clearly and with a loud enough tone so that you can be heard.

Be brief and be clear to the objective as to why you are calling. and remember the more calls you make the better you will ultimately get.

#4 I'm not available

Make sure to always call your customers even if they say the following.
- I'm flying out of town
- I'll be at work
- I have family coming into town this weekend

Call them anyway!

Things to remember

Before you call remember what their want and needs are prior to your call if you can figure out what they want you can use that later when they tell you no to guide them towards what you both want by suggesting your product and or service.

Customers need & want information to feel confident and comfortable

They want to find out if your product and or service can solve their problem or fulfill their desire based on the below 3 things

Information of course based on 3 things
    1. **Your product or service**
    2. **Your company**
    3. **You**

Once you have properly made your customer confident and comfortable on all 3 of these categories you will be able to close.

Distractions

It is okay to text clients while making calls on the phone to be productive and proactive. However, watching TV. in the background or having side conversations while trying to make calls can reflect in your conversation with the customer and prevent you from obtaining that appointment or deal.

In addition, make sure you're in the correct state of mind for that particular sales call for example if you're calling a customer who is in need of your service or product for financial reasons. Try to be a little empathic and understanding towards their particular situation. This does not mean to get side tracked and talk about fishing or camping, for 10 min. It means show them that you understand and care while guiding them towards your product or service.

By being in the right state of mind for your clients' needs and wants not only will it show you care but it will allow you to yield far better results for every sales call.

29 Laws of calling

1. Be in the right mindset of that call.
   This means putting yourself in the customer's scenario if you're calling somebody going through a divorce, maybe empathize, relate, understand, and provide a reliable solution.
2. Keep the sales process in mind, organize the call.
3. Do not get distracted talking about hunting or fishing. Stay focused. Remember the purpose of your call is one of four reasons.
   a. set an appointment
   b. sell a product or service
   c. obtain more business
   d. invite them guide them to something to read watch or do
4. Stay excited, be alive but not over the top.
5. This means be enthusiastic have excitement don't be dull but don't be so crazy that they consider you to be like every other salesman or worse. You scare them.
6. Captivate their attention fast
7. Everybody knows first impressions are everything, and when you're on the phone, the same is also true. You have to be interesting if you want people to find what you're saying interesting. So don't forget to use captivating tonalities, high- pitched low pitch and pauses when speaking.
8. Acknowledge
9. No matter what they say to you as to why they don't want to buy your product or service, make sure you repeat back to them, hey, I understand price is important to you.
10. Be honest and respectful.
11. Don't become emotionally upset if you hear a no. especially over the phone. Truthfully, your job as a salesperson does not even begin until a customer says no. If the customer always said yes, there would be no need for salespeople
12. Speak up and be clear
13. Create urgency, scarcity, and excitement all in one and then close for the appointment

14. The customer can see you on the other side of the phone be presentable
15. Most customers need information to feel confident and comfortable in moving forward with anything
16. Qualify quickly
17. Know your solution that you can provide to solve their problem
18. Be straight up
19. Recognize their objections and or problems
20. Appropriately handle objections
21. Remember, at the end of every script, have a call to action. A call to action is setting an appointment sending the customer a video or content to look over, or closing the sale or create your own call to action
22. Remember some people might be busy
23. Be brief
24. No, um hum, don't think out loud.
25. Take notes. Never know when you might have to repeat something back that you forgot or at your next meeting to impress them that you cared and were listening.
26. Never lie; instead, say: I don't know I'll find out.
27. Remember, you only have 5-7 seconds to captivate their attention. Once captivated, you can successfully deliver the rest of your call presentation.
28. Remember people have to feel comfortable and confident when making a decision.
29. Convince yourself everybody is a deal because most people need anywhere from 5 to 15 calls, text voicemails, videos watched. Ultimately people need the right information in order to make a decision.

Part Two

The Scripts

Script 1

Immediate Follow Up

Inside This Script

1. As soon as you receive an inbound lead, no matter what source, follow up immediately.

Remember:
Qualify quickly

Remember:
Know your solution that you can provide to solve their problem or to fulfill their desires

Remember:
Quickly Qualify

Sales Pro
Hello James, (Frank), with (XYZ) of (Los Angeles). You recently reached out indicating that you would like more information on our (Product or service)

Customer

Yeah, I'm interested in knowing more

Sales Pro
Allow me to ask you a question, why did you request information today?

Customer
I had time

Sales Pro
No, I mean, what got you wanting to get our (product or service) today?
(This question should allow you to discover their problem so you can guide them in a direction on the call with your product or solution)

Customer
Well, I'm going through a divorce, I got a job transfer, and my car payments are too high!

Sales Pro
I completely understand. I'm glad you reached out sounds like (lowering your car payments) is important to you and the sooner we can meet in person, the sooner we can talk about how we can possibly (lower your car payments).
James what's the earliest you can make it in?

Customer
I can make it in today at 4:30!

Sales Pro
Great, see you then!

Script 2

Second style Follow Up

Inside This Script

1. Is designed to qualify the customer and discover their hot points so that if needed later to set or close you can reinforce the customers decision by repeating back to them their hot buttons to move them towards taking a call to action.

Remember:
Qualify quickly

Remember:
organize the call & keep sale process moving it towards the Sale

---

Sales Pro
Hello James, this is (Frank) with (XYZ). The reason I'm calling is that you

requested to receive more information on (credit repair)? Do you mind if I ask you a few questions to make sure I'm not wasting your time?

Customer
Sure

Sales Pro
What is the number one reason why you want (to fix your credit)? What's most challenging when it comes to your (credit report)?
Why haven't you (fixed it) already?

Customer
Well, I want to fix my credit so that I can buy my family at home, and the biggest challenge I would say is my charged off debt, and I don't know how to remove it.

Sales Pro
What is the earliest we can meet so that we can start working towards (building your credit) so that you can purchase your family a home?

Customer
I'm free right now!

Script 3

My boss says, who do you know that wants to take advantage of this offer

Inside This Script

1. This scrip works better if you can offer a better deal to your customers for your product or service.

*Remember:
create urgency, scarcity, and excitement all in one and then close*

Sales Pro
Hey James, It's (Frank). Is this a good time to talk? I've got some great news!

Customer
Yes

Sales Pro
My boss just approached me and asked me if I knew anybody even remotely interested in using our (Product or service) To make sure I give them a call right away! And were going to make them a deal they simply can't refuse on (Product or service)

Customer
Wow, okay, what's going on?

Sales Pro
He says if we can meet today someway, somehow, you're going to get absolutely the best deal, however, I cannot make deals over the phone. You've got to get here in person to take advantage of it! What time can we meet today?

Customer
I'm at work, can't you just tell me what the deal is you have?

Sales Pro
Pretend for a second, you're the owner and you have 2 customer's one over the phone demanding what the deals are and the other customer in person demanding what the deals are, who would get the better deal? The customer over the phone or the customer in person?

Customer
Well, the customer in person, of course!

Sales Pro
That's exactly why I need you here. What time do you get off of work?

Customer
5 PM

Sales Pro
Okay, let's a set appointment for 6:15. Does that work for you, and do you remember how to get here?

Customer
Yes that works perfectly, and I also have the directions, thank you.

Sales Pro
I'm excited, I'll see you then.

Script 4

Leaving a Voice mail X4

Inside This Script

1. Contains four different styles of voicemails.

Remember:
the customer can see you on the other side of the phone so be presentable

---

Sales Pro
Great news:
Hello James, it's (Frank) with (XYZ) of (Los Angeles). I got some great news for you! You're going to want to call me back I'll give you my number. (123) 456-7890 Again, this is crazy call me back (123) 456-7890 it's (Frank) with (XYZ) I'll talk to you soon!

Customer
New product or service:
Hello James, this is (Frank) calling on number (123) 456-7890 with (XYZ) of (Los Angeles) I thought of you today because we just received this new (product

and/or service) that I know it will be a game changer for your (business/home/situation) you're going to love it! Again, this is (Frank) with (XYZ) call me back (123) 456-7890 So if you want to hear about it which I think you will call me back!

Sales Pro
Customer who will not move forward in your Sales process:
Hello James, it's (Frank) with (XYZ) we spoke briefly regarding (product or service) I'm hoping I can be the one to help you with your decision in moving forward. If you haven't made a decision by now, it's probably because there's a lack of information or lack of confidence in (me the product or service) call me back so we can figure out which one it is. I'm looking forward to helping you obtain that information and answer any questions that you may have, when you call me back. The number is (123) 456-7890 again it's (123) 456-7890

Sales Pro
Basic voicemail:
Hello James,
it's (Frank) with (XYZ) I'd like to speak to you briefly please call me at (123) 456-7890 again it's (Frank) with (XYZ) here's my number one more time (123) 456-7890 I'm excited and looking forward to your call back!

Script 5

Let's put a face to the name

Inside This Script

1. Your calling a customer who is interested and who has maintained communication but has not yet moved forward.

Remember:
most customers need information to feel confident and comfortable in moving forward with your sales process

---

Sales Pro
Hello James, it's (Frank) with (XYZ) of (Los Angeles).
As you know, we have spoken a few times I would like to put a face to the name. Can we meet later today for lunch?

Customer
Sure, if you're buying?

Sales Pro
My pleasure, what time do you typically take your lunch?

Customer
Around 12:30

Sales Pro
Okay, great how does (name of the restaurant) sound to you at 12:45?

Customer
That works, but I'm not buying anything when I'm there!

Sales Pro
I completely understand this is just a lunch meeting to go over your options. Besides, if it doesn't make 100% sense to you, it would be unethical if I asked you to (buy/use my product or service) besides, if anything, you get a free lunch out of it! I am Looking forward to our lunch,
I'll see you then.

Customer
Sounds good, thank you. I'll see you then.

Script 6

Circle of influence people that you know

Inside This Script

1. This is a call to your friend's family or customer fans.

Remember:
Be honest and respectful
Resourceful & Helpful

Sales Pro
Hey James, is this a good time to talk?

Customer
Yes

Sales Pro
James, who do you know looking to (Try/Use/My Product and or Service) in the next 30 days?

Customer
Nobody

Sales Pro
Okay, try to think about anybody in your Cell phone's contact list that (Needs/Can use My Product and or Service)

Customer
I cannot think of anyone

Sales Pro
Okay, No problem. do you remember anyone who complains or talks about having the worst (Related to my product or service) and wishes they could have (My Product and or service) Who comes to mind?

Customer
Lisa always talks about (XYZ)

Sales Pro
I know you wouldn't mind if I gave (her) a call. What is the number, I'm ready?

Customer
Her number is (123) 456-7890. That is everyone I can think of

Sales Pro
I really appreciate it. You're such a great friend, by the way. I'm sure after this conversation, you've decided that when you're ready to (Buy/Get my product or service) you're going to go through me, right?

Customer
Of course, because I can see your passionate about what you do.

Sales Pro
Great, what does your future (Related to my Product or service) Look like? (go into your qualifying questions)

Script 7

Take me off your call List

Inside This Script

1. This script is designed for after you deliver your offer, and the customer tells you take me off your call list. That is where this script would start.

Remember:
Be in the right mindset of that call

Customer
I am not interested. Please take me off your list……….

Sales Pro
John, I must say if I got a call out of the blue with somebody telling me about this, I probably ask to be taken off the list as well. I just really appreciate you taking the time out of your day to speak with me. I'll update the notes on my end,
Hey, while I got you on the phone, humor me for a second, you've heard the phrase before location, location, location, right?

Customer
Of course, everybody has.

Sales Pro
Well, in our business, it's all about timing, timing, timing, and usually when it's your time to (Sell/buy)(Sell) you're at the mercy of a (down market) and (low ball offers), I'm not asking you to make a decision based on this phone call alone, all I'm asking is an opportunity to sit down with you to show you how we can make this a win-win situation for both of us! So if you were to take advantage of this (up market) and I'm not saying that you are, would you be looking to (sell) for ($550,000 or more like $600,000)?

Customer
Well, of course, the $600,000

Sales Pro
Okay, great, I'm going to need (30minutes) to (touch and feel the property) to see if it is possible. If it takes any longer, it is because you like what you hear. Will you make time to meet with me today?

Customer
Sure I can do that

Script 8

Elevator script, A.K.A. asking for sales anywhere

Inside This Script

1. Remember no matter where you are people are more likely to do business with people who do business with them.

Remember:
Be Clear

Remember:
Captivate their attention fast

Sales Pro
Excuse me, can I ask you a question?

Customer
Sure, what's up

Sales Pro
Do you currently (rent or own your home)?

Customer
I rent. Why?

Sales Pro
If you could (own your home) for the same price you're (renting), would you consider it?

Customer
Well yeah, of course, I would love to own

Sales Pro
Great, what is your cell phone number? (Look down at your cell phone as you ask this question as if you are typing into your phone already)

Customer
(123) 456-7890

Sales Pro
Great and your name and email?

Script 9

Are you selling?

Inside This Script

1. In this script you are cold calling somebody's property or product that you wish to acquire. So that you can replace it with your new product or service.

Remember:
some people might actually be busy

Sales Pro
Hello, John
This is (Frank) from (XYZ) of (Los Angeles). I'm calling because we have (active buyers/Great offers) for those looking to (buy Property/ or upgrade their current Product) in the (12345) Zip Code. To be sure, I'm not wasting your time. Let me ask you a question to see if your (Property/Current Product) qualifies?

Customer
Okay

Sales Pro
Is there any reason you haven't (listed/sold upgraded) your (Property/Product/Service) already?

Customer
Yes, because we're not interested in doing that.

Sales Pro
I understand you're not interested in (selling/upgrading) however if you received an offer so big to where It stopped you dead in your tracks! Would you consider it?

Customer
Probably... How much are we talking?

Sales Pro
Okay hold on John other than yourself, who would have to be involved in this decision?

Customer
My wife

Sales Pro
Will you make time for me tomorrow to meet with you and your wife so I can show you exactly what I'm talking about?

Customer
Sure, we can do that!

Script 10

Second Sale

Inside This Script

1. They already said yes to the first sale.
2. They already like and trust you.

Remember:
Stay excited be alive but not over the top

Remember:
some Stay brief

Sales Pro
Hey John, what's up? This is (Frank) with (XYZ). How are you doing?

Customer
Hey Frank,
How's it going, man? Everything is great. The family loves the (the new product or

service that we got for my wife!)

Sales Pro
Great, man I'm glad to hear that. That's actually why I'm calling you. When we were (looking at products and services) together, I noticed that you likes the (X product), and this morning I noticed that a brand new (X product) arrived today, and I'd personally like to drive over to you so you can try it on. Are you home now?

Customer
Yes, we are home, but I'm not buying anything. I just purchased a brand new (X product) for my wife.

Sales Pro
I completely understand you just bought a brand new (X product) for your wife and I am grateful for your business. I'm coming over to you on my dime. I'm going to give you a fantastic (X product) presentation and let you demo it for free and its gonna take 20 minutes if I'm there any longer. It's because you like what you see.

Customer
Of course, I'm going to like what I see. Well, okay, come by but I'm not buying anything, we are making lunch. Hope you're hungry?!

Sales Pro
I am I'll see you soon.

Script 11

Let's see if we can save you money

Inside This Script

1. This script is designed to upgrade a current client on a product or service or to obtain new business

Remember:
Keep the sales process in mind & organize the call in the direction of a call to Action

---

Sales Pro
Hello, this is (Frank) with (XYZ). The reason why I'm calling is that there's a strong possibility that our company could save you (a couple hundred dollars a month on your product or service) payment! To be certain that I don't waste your time, let me ask you a question?

Customer
Okay, what is it

Sales Pro
When was the last time you? (upgraded/ refinanced/ your property or service)?

Customer
We never have before.

Sales Pro
Okay, sounds like there is another decision maker involved. Am I correct?

Customer
Yes, there is two of us on the paperwork or our (product or Service)

Sales Pro
Okay great, If I can deliver on the kind of results that I'm talking about with you, would you be willing to schedule an appointment with me? If so, when are you and the other decision maker available?

Customer
Later, this evening at six works for us, that's when my wife will be home.

Sales Pro
Okay, great I'll talk to you then.

Script 12

Why haven't you purchased our product or service yet?

Inside This Script

1.This script is for a customer who has not moved forward with doing business with you yet and they keep throwing reasons why they can't do business.

Remember:
Recognize their objections and or problems and then elegantly provide a solution your solution is your service offer or product

---

Sales Pro
Hello Barbara,
(Frank), with (XYZ). The reason I'm calling is to ask why you haven't (traded in /bought our product/used our service) yet?

Customer
I don't have enough information on it/I need to sleep on it/it cost too much!

Sales Pro
Okay I understand (it cost too much/you don't have enough information/you need to sleep on it)
To be sure I'm not wasting your time, let me ask you. If you were able to just magically (Trade in your Car/upgrade your service/ use our product instead) without your current monthly expenditure changing. What would you get?

Customer
Well, I would definitely get a brand new (Product or service) to fit my family's needs)

Sales Pro
Okay, great what day can we schedule an appointment for you and your family to come into the (office/store/dealership) to see if we can make this happen for you?

Customer
Is it going to cost the same? Because I can't afford anything more than I'm paying now.

Sales Pro
First, let's make sure that the New (product or service) even fits your family's needs and that you like the way it (handles and feels) because if that doesn't make sense, then there's no sense in even talking about the cost. As far as the cost goes, if it is not 100% affordable to you down to the penny, you can tell me no. What day can I meet you and your family?

Customer
This Saturday at 10 AM works well for us we'll see you there.

Sales Pro
Perfect, I'm excited I'll have the (Product/ Service) ready to go for you and your family!

Script 13

In home presentation or B2B Presentation

Inside This Script

1. You are seeking an in-person presentation

No um, hum, or maybes & do not think out loud

Remember:
If you don't know something say I don't know, but I'll find out NEVER lie

---

Sales Pro
Hello James
(Frank) (XYZ) of (Los Angeles), how are you? I'll be in the area of (North Los Angeles). I'd like to come by see you and give you and your (family/business/staff/ employees) a free presentation. There's no money involved. It"ll take 20 minutes.
I'm going to give you and your (family/ business/staff/employees) a free (Name of Product/Service) presentation, and it'll cost you nothing!

Customer
I'm not interested/were not interested

Sales Pro
I understand, of course you're not interested.
Why would you be. You don't even know what I'm going to present at your (home/business) and what I'm going to present at your (home/business) is I'm going to show you exactly how to (save 49% on your current product/service bill!/(Increase your business 49%!) How many (homes/businesses do you have?)

Customer
We have two homes/ two businesses

Sales Pro
How about I (save you $1,000 in 20 minutes! (Get you 50 more clients in 20 minutes

Customer
How do I do That!

Sales Pro
Can you make time for me to meet with you tomorrow?

Customer
Yes I can do that, lets meet.

Script 14

Customer is comparing the competition

Inside This Script

1. Never say anything bad about the competitor.

Remember:
at the end of every script have a call to action

Sales Pro
Hello John, this is (Frank) from (XYZ) do you have a minute?

Customer
Yes, I do

Sales Pro
Great the purpose of my call is to ask you if you've decided to move forward with our (Product or service)?

Customer
No not yet because I'm comparing other products/services.

Sales Pro
OK, great what (product/services are you comparing)?

Customer
I'm looking at the X product the Y product and the Z product.

Sales Pro
Those are all good choices but let me ask you something. It seems like my (product/service) meets all your needs and wants am I correct?

Customer
Yes. However, I just want to make sure I'm getting the best deal.

Sales Pro
I completely understand it sounds like price is important to you just like all my (customers/clients).

Customer
It is!

Sales Pro
I'll tell you what. Shopping and comparing can be exhausting so here's what we're going to do let's set up a day we can meet to revisit the (product/service) to re validate it is in fact what you want and while your here if the (product/service) is not 100% affordable , to where you say "OK I'll take it!". I'll kick you out of the (office/store/dealership) myself and drop you off at the competitor.
What day can we meet?

Customer
I can come in right now if you can do that!

Sales Pro
I'll see you soon.

Script 15

Asking for Referrals X 4

Inside This Script

1. This is when you planted a seed early on that you will be asking for referrals from your client down the road.

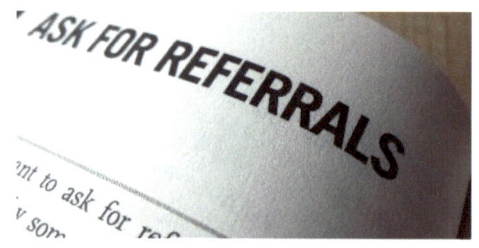

Remember:
Appropriately Handle objections when selling

---

1 of 4
Sales Pro
Hey John, it's (Frank),
Just checking in and touching base to see how you love your new (product/service)? and to see if there's any questions that I can have answered for you?

Customer
You're the man, thank you so much for getting me and my family this new(product/service). Everything is great. How are you?

Sales Pro

Well, John, As you know, (inventory) is (low) right now, and I have a (buyer/seller) that would like to (buy/sell in your (neighborhood/area) I was wondering who you might know that may be looking to (sell/buy) in your area?

Customer
Well my neighbors came over and we were talking, and they mentioned that they might be planning on (buying/selling) soon.

Sales Pro
Great, that sounds good. What are their names and numbers? (end of 1 of 4)

2 of 2
Sales Pro
Hey John,
it's Frank I'm just calling to touch base to see if there's any questions I can have answered for you I know getting familiar and learning a new (product and/or service) can create a lot of questions and I just want to make sure that you know how to use it perfectly?

Customer
No, I had a question, but I figured it out I love it thank you for helping me upgrade!

Sales Pro
That is good to hear. Hey John can you help me out! let me ask you, do you have any friends or family members or coworkers who want or would like to have any of the (products or services) that I represent?

Customer
I cannot think of anyone

Sales Pro
I understand, who do you know that really needs to (upgrade) their (product/service) because it 'super old?

Customer

Now that you mention it Bob has a really old (product/service) and he talks about upgrading it every day because people bother him about it. I'll text you Bob's number.

Sales Pro
Great thank you! (end of 2 of 4)

Script 16

Asking for Referrals continued

Inside This Script

1. It's important to know that most customers mentioned that they would give a referral if asked.

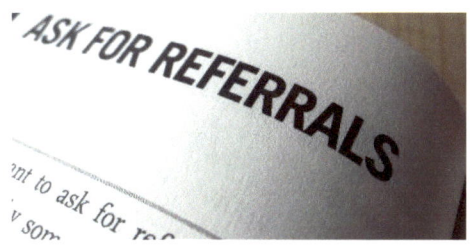

Remember:
Be in the right mindset of that call

Sales Pro
Hey John, it's (Frank) just touching base here, how are you? How's the (product and or service)?

Customer
Hey Frank, everything is great man we love it thank you so much!

Sales Pro
Hey John, can I get your help with something? I'm planning a client appreciation event and I'm taking a poll and I'd like to know what you personally suggest here are some ideas. Idea 1 Idea 2 what do you think? Do you have any ideas or

suggestions?

Customer
I like all the ideas. I'll definitely be there.

Sales Pro
I'm excited you'll be there, also feel free to invite anybody who might show similar interest in these (products and or services). It is going to be a lot of fun, and we will have food and prizes!
(end of 3 of 4)

4 of 4
Sales Pro
Hey John, it's (Frank), how's everything going?

Customer
Everything is great, man, how have you been?

Sales Pro
Well, as you know, we had a great time working together. It was a lot of fun! I know I want to do business with people who want to do business with me. I also like to do business with people that I like, and I also know that likeness surrounds with likeness, so that got me wondering. Who do you know that's like you that may want to use the (Product and or service) that I represent?

Customer
My neighbor Tom

Sales Pro
Great, what's Tom's last name, and his phone number, and why do you think Tom would be interested? (end of 4 of 4)

Script 17

Calling referrals

Inside This Script

1. You are calling a referral that one of your prospects or customers gave you

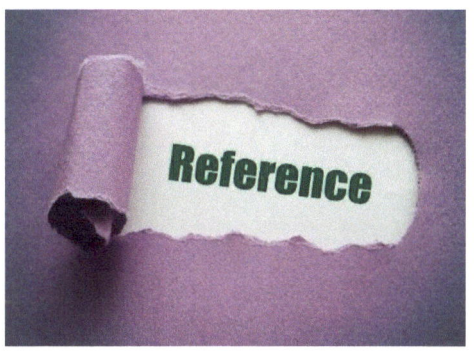

Remember:
Appropriately handle objections

Sales Pro
Hey James!
(Frank) here with (XYZ) looks like we have a common contact Bob. By the way, he just (Bought/Used/Our Product and or Service) and he loves it!

Customer
Good for him! /I am not interested!

Sales Pro
Bob told me you that you would say no. And he also insisted at the very minimum

that I absolutely must show you what we are doing for so many (Families/People/Businesses) and that you personally must see how it (Solved their Problem/ Saved/ Created/ Made Money/ enhanced their business/sold their home quickly/whatever your product or service does.)

For yourself! So when can (I get 30 min of your time/we meet in person/ you come to the office/ I come over)? To show this to you?

Customer
Fine, this Friday works.

Sales Pro
Okay Do you prefer mornings? Afternoons? Or Evenings?

Customer
Mornings around 10 AM works

Sales Pro
Okay, Great, I'll See you then! (Confirm Address, location, time, Etc.)

Script 18

Recruitment

Inside This Script

1. Always lead the conversation.

*Remember:
Captivate their attention fast*

Sales Pro
Hello, John (Frank) with (XYZ) of (Los Angeles),
I'm calling because I focus on seeking out highly functional talented individuals and determining whether or not they would be a good fit for our company. Do you have a moment?

Customer
Yes, I do

Sales Pro

Great, I'm excited, we're going to streamline the traditional, over the phone process. Can you make time to meet with me this week to determine if we would be a good fit for each other?

Customer
That sounds good I can meet this Thursday at 1 o'clock.

Sales Pro
That works I'll see you then

Script 19

Recruitment continued

Inside This Script

1. It is important not to sound desperate when making a recruiting call.
2. You're merely trying to see if both you and the potential job candidate would make a great fit.

Remember:
Qualify quickly

Sales Pro
Hello John, this is (Frank) from (XYZ). Do you have a minute?

Customer
Yes, I do

Sales Pro
The purpose of my call is that your resume looks like it may fit with our expectations as an organization. I'd like to sit down in front of you to see if you'd be a good fit. What day this week can we make this happen?

Customer
I'm free anytime

Script 20

Reset an appointment that was canceled

Inside This Script

1. Don't make your customer feel bad for canceling the initial appointment.

Remember:
Know your solution that you can provide to solve your customer's problem

---

Sales Pro
Hey, James, it's (Frank) with (XYZ). As you know, we missed our Appointment?

Customer
I had a doctor's appointment come up sorry about that.

Sales Pro
Hey, I understand, and I know life happens. I also know that this (Product or service) is important to you.

Customer
Yeah, that's the thing I'm not sure yet if it's for me.

Sales Pro
Sounds like you don't have enough information to make a decision.

Customer
Your right I don't.

Sales Pro
Well the biggest part of my job is to provide information, that will help you determine if this (Product or service) is right for you or not. So, in order for me to do that, I'll need about (30 minutes) of your time. If takes any longer than that, it's because you like what you hear. What's the best day we can do that?
Are you free today?

Customer
Today at 6 works

Sales Pro
Okay, just to confirm today at 6 PM, we will meet at (XYZ) location. Is there any reason under the sun that you can think of that would prevent you from NOT making our apartment today at 6 PM?

Customer
No nothing. I'll for sure be there!

Sales Pro
Great see you then.

About the author

Frank Bravo – The Ardent Salesman!

Frank started his sales journey working for a retail clothing store. At first, he was working for his employer in the early 4 AM morning shipment shifts, and there he saw a well-dressed man passing by, with an aura and personality that Frank couldn't shrug off. He immediately wanted to know him, and what he was doing there so early. Frank asked his retail boss who that man was and without hesitation his boss took Frank to her office, as she knew the man. The man was one of the District Loss Prevention Managers of that retail company and she introduced them to each other. Frank blurted out without hesitation that he would be honored to work for him. Indeed, it was his lucky day, as the introduction changed into a conversation, and then into an interview, and later that week, Frank was working for him as a Loss Prevention Agent. With passion and determination, anything is possible, and that was a working element in his life as he was promoted to a Loss Prevention Agent. Soon, he became one of the top Loss Prevention Agents of the San Francisco region. The only way Frank could stop a shoplifter was to convince them with his words, since this company had a hand's off Policy. While he was undergoing new self-realization, he found himself talking and convincing shoplifters to come back into the store, where most authorities would be waiting to take action. He found out that he can persuade people very quickly, and people listened to him intently. Undeniably it was a natural gift, and realization that dawned on him that he can do wonders with it. His first instinct was to use his gift for sales.

Frank was enthusiastic about cars growing up, so he instinctively decided to sell cars and join a car sales dealership. Surely, working with professionals is a grand and enlightening learning experience. In his first month, he got his training, and Frank often says, what he learned in that first month will stay with him as a skill forever. Later he started working at the capacity, and he was working every minute of his shift without breaks. Maybe that became the reason for two drastic fold of events. For one, he sold twenty-seven cars in his first full month and landed himself a fat paycheck.

Later by the end of the month, he was fired for conducting the sales without a veteran while he was still in his training phase. The very next day, he decided to take this energy forward positively, by learning from the mistakes. Soon he was at the door of the biggest car sales dealership of the that city, in neat, primed clothes with his resume in hand. Since he was out there to prove himself, he landed the job, and this time around, he was cautioned and aimed for harmony in life. Owing to the manager of that place, who believed in an immature in the field, Frank started generating sales. With the staff that lifted each other up and celebrated each other's victories, Frank soon learned a lot and felt like a differently stable and sound person. Frank soon was the go to person around his friends and family for advice, and he often was giving ideas to friends family and strangers on how to approach situations and ask for anything that they would want in life and to tackle it till the goal post, just like sales.

One day at the dealership he was working for, during the training, the coach stated a fact, that 9 out of 10 sales people won't make it past 90 days and that indeed was the truth, from what he has seen in his years of service. Frank realized there had been a-lot of good men and women who he really enjoyed working with, but for whatever reason they never made it. So, he gradually started training new salesman that came to the dealership, and several months later during a training, it was surprising to see all the individuals he has trained have sustained, and this time around, more than half the number stayed. Well, that indeed was an eye-opening experience and a transitioning reflection for him, and he realized with deliberation and calculation, he had formulated a pattern for people to follow.

With that purpose in mind, he started writing down all the trainings he passed on to new salesman in the dealership. After some time, he had compiled a gift for all new salespeople who are out there. He had made his phone strategies and word tracks available in this book, for everyone to read and learn. as he has seen himself, train many individuals and watched them implement his strategies and are now successfully achieving results. Frank aims that he could make a little difference in salespeople's lives by helping them make more sales and earn a better living for them and their families. The idea of giving back to society is very content and exhilarating for him.

www.ingramcontent.com/pod-product-compliance
Lightning Source LLC
Chambersburg PA
CBHW041526090426
42736CB00035B/17